TELESCOPE HIGHWAY

TONI SIMON

ISBN 978-1-956005-20-2

Library of Congress Cataloging-in-Publication Data
Names: Simon, Toni, author. | Mennipus (Spirit)
Title: Telescope Highway / Toni Simon.
Description: New York City : Spuyten Duyvil, [2021] |
Identifiers: LCCN 2021039895 | ISBN 9781956005202 (paperback)
Subjects: LCGFT: Experimental poetry.
Classification: LCC PS3619.I56265 T45 2021 | DDC 818/.609--dc23
LC record available at https://lccn.loc.gov/2021039895

TELESCOPE HIGHWAY

TONI SIMON

spuytenduyvil

NEW YORK CITY

Special thanks and appreciation to
Nick Piombino and Beryl Simon for their
assistance with editing, thanks to Kim Lyons and
Maria Damon for their support, Margery Meadow for
proofreading, and Anne Noonan for design.

Sections of Telescope Highway first appeared
in Ping Pong 2013, Drunken Boat 16, M/E/A/N/I/N/G:
The Final Issue, Chant de la Sirene: Black Friday
Election 2016 and Boog City Reader 7.

Thanks to editors Joanna Fuhrman,
Kristin Prevallet, Susan Bee and Mira Schor,
Laura Hinton and Nicole Peyrafitte.

CONTENTS

UPRISING

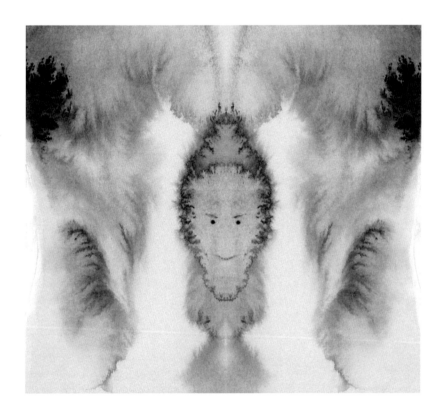

*Menippus: I saw all this, the life of man came before me under
the likeness of a great pageant arranged and marshaled by Chance,
who distributed infinitely varied costumes to the performers.*
— Lucian of Samosata, *The Book of Necromancy* c.165 AD

Angels swept past the ark in search of distant thunder. After the deluge it was said that Hercules fell backwards before meeting his maker. Cups of wine overflowed with grief but this was not the day to lament.

For among the wrinkles of time there dwelt a golden princess who eclipsed the sun. The world was in flames (our place in the world should arrive shortly). An acidic meltdown, between the cracks of frosty fuel.

Elfin heretics recalled the missing meritocracy, for there was at this time a misguided plutocrat who ruled the world of things with his immaculate ideology. In the hidden territories of the back-channeled they could evade the authorities at the other end of the rainbow. Somewhere inside the district was a narrow escape and inside the escape was a narrower escape — inside that lingering fear. This crinkle in time had no blueprint.

In the year of deflected materialized terror
people carried tremor guides.

From inside the insensitive beehive
an occult wakeup call to administer the theremin
as they trembled before the herd.

Whistleblowers caught the time lapse train to nowhere,
and Armageddon informants turned gelatinous
before the miniature Machiavellians.

The larks are inheriting the frost the dew collects on the unemployment lines. Escape at the end the rainbow is underhanded. In the towns the cities are seething, leaden masses too hot to handle. Traditional structures are dividing and conquering the will of the people. Termites set in and delay the foundations from crumbling by careful re-examination with their teeth. No home entertainment guides, due to lack of discretion. In bleachers the onlookers are not scorned for wearing plaid, they are too busy with the popcorn to indicate their weariness. Uniformness is betrayed too soon by blowing glass from the wrong dimension.

By inducing euphoria the circle evolved into a wheel until there was no more reason to return. Harping on the same moments became a pastime, occurring in a past when there was no record of emotions. The wheel gets knocked around and can no longer spin. The free world survives on such allusions. Only the thoughts are crumbling and disintegrating without glue to cohere them. Silence invades the crevices of sanity and holds its own — to resist means death. Do not remove underwear from our monuments or step over the yellow line of delusion. Dark powers invade newspapers and merge with crimes well spent as a day on the beach. Up ahead a carrot waves in the breeze, an airy promise.

Clouds of misgiving settle on the populace. The air raid shelters are full up. Some wag a finger at authority and question its foundations. Others seek progression in a waterfall of clay idols before succumbing to the mass directives. Fomenting anger cannot distinguish the inhabitants from one another. In a litany of monologues the head swells and reveals an assortment of shells. Mollusks fly out of ears and leap towards the horizon, fulfilling the ancient prophecy.

Arkansas whispers "activate the negotiation chip,"
and negotiates away the active corridor to memory lane.
Ride a magic carpet to the fatalistic future swap,
costumed for the infinite war.
They think the alternate universe is out to get them for no
apparent reason (perhaps the vortex missed the boat to Bethlehem).
Believe in a 6,000 year old chewable world.

Telemarketers to the stars recount the golden blossoms of Ur. In
the maker's cabin the wingless beast is a mannequin's nightmare.
A graffiti outpost lies concealed inside a telegram (it's not what's
inside, but what is revealed by your forebearers to be real and true
that continues on). Afterwards they float into your archetypal drone,
smarter than a hellion's gate, and more lethal.

The characters are not what they seemed in their previous world.
An apparition recalls its original state, the time when ancient
messengers returned to the fallen estuary, their indigo tails glowed
brightly as hybrid mentalists reclaimed a code lost to the ages.

Mercurial doubt flakes overtake the marching fairy tales. Translucent highway shimmers before the throne of forgotten Jericho. The hermaphrodite scrolls down the alleyway. An incandescent glimmer surrounds the television Terpsichore in a toga. Wistful Medusa leads the Pegasus parade, exiting the warped rotunda. A Chiron refusnik crosses the river on his own sticks, the other side teeming with messenger frenzy.

Seen through a small keyhole, the harbinger misanthrope hides behind the Aristotelian arcade.

Airtight window on the eternal epigram spells interior product control. Barcode Madonna decries messiah backlash when foresight brings the carpenter to the apocalypse.

This story is about the connection between the before and after. We talk tomorrow today. Exchanger expedites with Moses bundles, the exchangers of the curtain times most enterprising illusion. Whodunit clause for Barnacle Sam. Detective swallows alleged email apostle; remembers Rumsfeld's ancient aspartame formaldehyde air suit fireside chat.

Orbits swirl in time. Instant apocalypse betrays the weary. We anticipate a world full of nuclear horror yet somehow this will all fade away.

Detained at the border of catastrophe our heroine seeks immensity's doppelganger, carrying only hyphenated spears. She locates a subterranean vestibule before bidding farewell.

It's Victorian tea time!

With record temperatures, from arid cliffs, she motions for a winged saint to descend and hand over the goods. Clouds of diaphanous wings descend on Telescope Highway for the missile launch countdown. A military spokesman relocated to the end time, carries the capitalists to the mountain reborn.

The narrowness of her escape will become legendary fodder for the lingering remains. Having evaded the eye of the windowless room she finds the escape hatch under the landing zone of the future. And appearing within, hidden in a package, the thread, and a mesmerization mirror.

She dreams of symbols projected on transparent screens. They reveal a future where cyborgs can utilize kryptonite materialization prototypes to evade Heisenberg motion detectors. At the meringue portal they look for an escalator to the wormhole — but its screen is molten on both sides. Barrier pigeons detect a force field — an experimental nose ring broadcast equipage.

When there's a time it will tell:

Twinkle, ambivalent atom, twinkle on demand

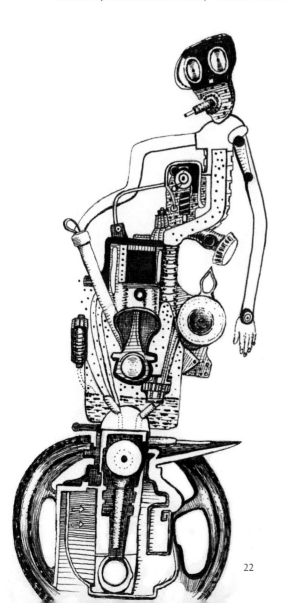

The zones of the future are bound by invisible chains to a world full
of illusion. Miniature reveries are caught off course, bent and folded
in an alien fashion. Inside the well inside of being and covertly
covered by fields, the matter of time is concrete and more real than
the mirage ahead of us.

Within their beds the dormant lie opposed to the central idea. Clear
the air of smoky residue before a coating of soot spreads evenly
throughout the world. Regain a trace of wisp in the inches of empty
space. Once past forever done.

A salute to certainty opens behind a cloud.

The moment subsides as the future takes over unannounced; the previous meaning overthrown by an arbitrary coup. Marching forward tomorrow's lessons fly in on the arrows of yesterday's fleeting solidity. The old ideas ferment in golden urns. They say in times past expression watered the vestibule goddess; now undone the tale's spent silos reveal a carved monogram. Like a stack of cards once folded and then forgotten, a deck without a suit to wear, clothed in finery before all the gods.

An anchor attaches itself to an industrial waste site, reducing protective deities to ribbon serenades. Having fallen into the river of soot they float around before stepping on shore.

Capitalistic curtains profit by the hunters' prey. Misty platitudes go a-courtin' after harlequin miasma directs diamonds outward towards cliché.

Dilapidated halos require our maintenance. Demons invade our bodies, lying down on our desks to slowly curl and wilt. Raisin-coated junkie streets follow the thread like songs out of salt shakers. A platitude syringe found wasted by the roadside squalor. They turn back and walk the narrow precipice of intended consequences, bending to the will of the past, recording their last words in a dusty folder.

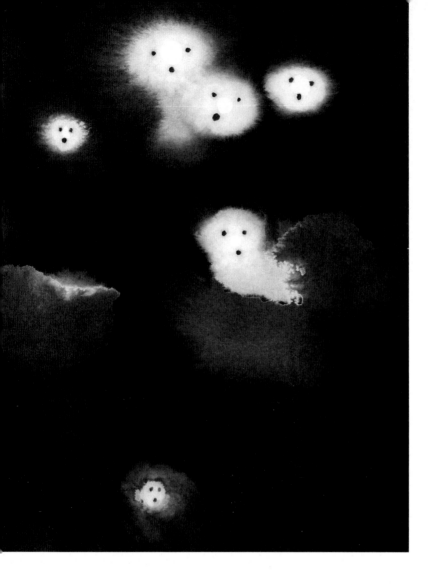

The old tales say that in a twilight hour the werewolf wheels took wing. Ectoplasm enveloped the vernacular.

Through darkened time tunnel detours the backwards clock rang the bell home, tearing out the invisible threading of the past.

Whistle for the many departed from earth.

Instant recall reminded the raven of the invisible web we locate ourselves in. But it's not forever where the dark increments are stored. In the extinct pathways of yore there was a man swelled by the precariousness he perceived in the ether around him. He sought worldwide recognition but without an inkling as to how, mistaking his identity for a wagon followed by a horse.

It was once said that thought is a bubble world of solitude. A glimmer of carapace spied inside the distant bubble, a winged vessel carrying the emperor's stick over the bridge to the suspended island.

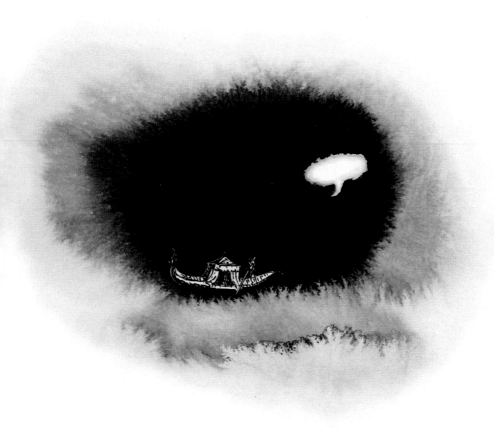

The king withholds crinkle time
Weeping princess punditry and her perfect puppetry forebearers
declare it's invertebrate polka time
Archaic mentors return to the muffled afternoon
turning cryptic crayons into dust
chase toy mirage

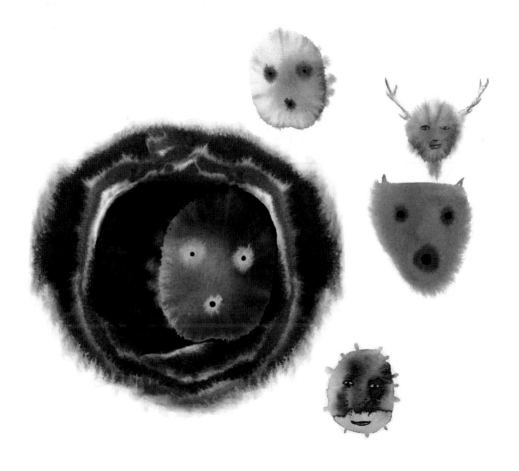

Fortune resembles a forlorn wayfarer struggling blindly over a barren terrain. From the sands she sprouts mechanical offspring; seeks a camel with exhaust pipe dreads for experimental reality drones. If you catch the drifting machines they will line up and salute the haze.

Paranoids tinfoil the multitudes and carry them over the dell. A voice warns: *never enter the merry-go-round backwards when anticipating a menacing storm.*

Utopian trailer park reveals a secret alias
"preamble's courtier"
Expect to receive an invisible partner
Carousel of pleasure evades the trolley's intractable charter
Change was forever as mercury slides a triple cartwheel
Archway to the celestial afterwards
Time is a slippery, silvery serpent this tinsel town minute

Space is a perpendicular appointment with destiny
and destiny is what remains outside the door
waiting to be delivered.

ODYSSEY

*Menippus: I resolved to go to Babylon and ask help from one of
the Magi, Zoroaster's disciples and successors; I had been told that by
incantations and other rites they could open the gates of Hades, take down
any one they chose in safety, and bring him up again... When he thought
me sufficiently prepared, he took me at midnight to the Tigris, then made a
magic circle round me to protect me from ghosts, and finally led me home
backwards just as I was; it was now time to arrange our voyage.*
— Lucian of Samosata, *The Book of Necromancy* c.165 AD

The story is sung in many ways. She was never sure of where she came from but would like to find her way home. War, famine and disease abound and it is difficult to find a way out. She is looking for shelter amid the turmoil. At the entrance to the Telescope Highway she detects a principle discovery fork.

Focus on a limited horizon and the glass will appear redacted. Stars appear as pinpoints of infinity, the sun as a golden magnet, the moon a reflective well leading all the way to China. Beneath the ground insect stamina provides a ballast for earth's rotating sphere.

Somewhere beyond the door to the aquarium armory lies the distant ocean, a wavering redundancy. Here, amidst uncertainty, she sets sail.

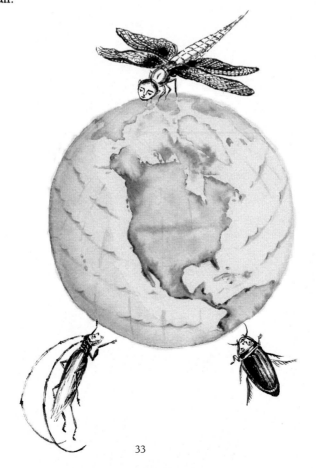

It was then that I first recognized my character for what she was. It was difficult to remain afloat at that time in the sea of so much turmoil. Advisable to float beforehand and sink the decks later, seafarers are seldom risked for their own good. The phone rang at just the right moment and the receiver was blue from the waist down. Too many times had passed and not much was said. It is claimed "all good things must end" but insufficient evidence to conjure up the past. The places gone are imaginative slices in the main pie, to serve in the guise of events.

In secret they prepare their gifts. It's the dawn of a first day but what is its intention? To touch base with finer motives would disguise the light appearing before her in the shape of melancholy.

"Reflections turned the mirror sideways." Reminders of the past dance before her eyes, the meaning obscured behind billowing folds. To outlast the will is to undertake a long journey — onward there's a point of succession.

A hidden force has risen.

Below the earth are rings of falling stars, they sleep with the ages. Rotating wheels, and fortune the goblet. Encased in plastic stereo siding, hiding the etiquette of swarms.

In the time of the pharaohs an hourglass melted into a thousand years.

Climbing forward past broken monuments, a rock astray had finer thoughts — manifested ironies by subtle approach. Tiptoeing in on backward glances she was struck by its honesty. The stars would not reveal their source while all the world was waiting.

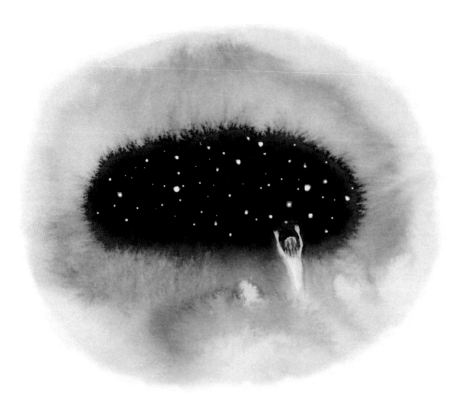

The sky was an open onion formation. A starry night was alone, disguised in a hermetic glow, all traces of its being removed. The road was long before and could not be retraced. She was somewhere in the middle of this twinkling and could not be persuaded. It had to do with the way the hangings were torn, the way they faced each other in global communication.

Outwardly she strives to appear calm but benumbed by misfortunes she throws her net into the vast ocean for remnants once cast aside. She finds them on similar shores and awaits the conclusion. Seeing the despair of too much trying, a crystallized mind faceted by pain. Tripping over one rock after another, cares are worn in this fashion, but light radiates from within. The sadness comes from knowing its departure, it will not stand unaided.

The many traditional crossings mar her view. She searches for a hidden expression and out of the blue it appears. She could view the world and it would not evade her grasp. Pain is the driving wheel, under nails it proceeds forward. Exclusion, a solemn theme, the surrounding wires and nails form an impenetrable crust.

Negative assumptions conclude in distant lands. A fool's errand to the masters' gate. Forced into limbo the outcasts turn inward, return and are forced outwards. In falling snow, losses are recovered and the interested parties resume once again. The shoe fits the wrong foot, it outlasts the wearer. Sleep cannot be found. Inside the crack of dawn she searches through its corridor but empty footsteps bring no peace. The wrong building altogether (sleep the elusive and capricious slave seeks to free itself and go its own way). Anxiety wavers and assumes grand proportions, it consumes.

Torch is to flame what increment holds before a mirror.

She is caught up in a dilemma. Though striving for a careful
solution, the roads are blocked by rioting trees. No sooner
finished when caught once again in a new wave of circumstance,
forfeiting her ability to speak coherently. Cherishing her freedom
undercurrents abound.

She bounds through a maze of deterring factors. The victims are laid waste by recalling the old tunes and flavor their tea with bitter herbs once remembered. Only time can tell the outcome; it waits around the corner of perception knowing you will catch up with your shadow when the time presents itself. A lost and found object which will only fade.

A judgment is made and rules are broken. The queen announces her
arrival, she can't wait to be seated with the rest. A far-flung thought
reveals its inherent source. We hang around the bar waiting for the
last round — acceptable behavior shuns us in public. There's no
explanation for these constant imaginings. Characters appear out of
books when we least expect them.

A kitchen is folded by a mouse into suitable quarters. It occupies
the landing by transmuted pain. Time seeks out a quality it cannot
pursue openly. It surrounds the hours and only ceases its search
when there is no more substance left to eat. Characteristics of an
active atom. Galvanized forces in an open march.

Intention creates the will to succeed. It is said the road twists and turns in many ways, created out of time and traveling beyond its realm. She ventures into solitude and reflects. Vicarious as she is her direction becomes clear. She knows her limits and will follow them to the end. She was forewarned. There is no certainty, only relation.

The moment yields its course; thoughts reflected in silver stream. Apparent purpose shifts towards an awakening. Out of this it diverges and follows a different probability. Tributaries to a verbal trace. The moment loses its significance but recaptures its direction. Visible futures carried onwards and down the river are united.

The earth's song still echoes through endless canyons. In after-thought the way was a timeless stretch of meaning visited by the spirit. Once the path was a clear and simple choice, we had only ourselves to pursue. As we proceed the outside world drops its veneer and seeks to entertain. Nearing the approach the gate is not locked.

The future grows in its retreat from the past. If only we could be told in advance but indications call forth the opposite. Apprehended at the border they seek to redeem themselves. Climbing the narrow passageway there is no room for acceptance; other doctrines justify its existence. Outside her window there is no footing. It is apparent the dawn is beginning; coupons insure its progress. Indications of a storm and sleep are upon us; safely inside now as the winds rage outside the door and seagulls walk a promenade paved with shells. Perhaps she's already proceeded too far, unaware of their presence. All at once she opens her door and views the obvious.

AFTERMATH

The future will contain all the filaments of the past. Robots will insist on inclusion. Our minds will jellify, like thoughts in a curtain call implosion.

Now the folds of time unfold to the present. She comes home and proffers a jar of traditional substance into a jar of traditional meaning. Just the intimation of fluidity could result in a crease in magnetic time. But to distance oneself from that octopus requires byzantine reflection, and not wholly suited to the wrinkles of the hours and minutes we create to appease the god of reason.

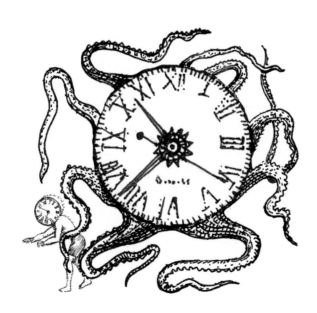

Erebus, lord of the underworld, mixes the heart and measures the
mind's elemental ethers. Miniature metropolis within his hand
wishes for a misbegotten future world. Archaic molds of withering
leaves recalled whenever the flies come home, and once recalled a
window opens to the waiting room dream. The precipice dissolves
into sugar cubes of thought in time for the ethereal mission. A
figure would sit on the world of tomorrow without blinking an
eye. It doesn't know its sequel, dissolving before the stone gods
it aspires to reproduce. A warlock imagines himself in a golden
wedding gown. He harbors illusions of an internal sun, before the
approaching storm.

Reticence never becomes the flower and the misanthrope will never rescue the fly from the batter. The soldiers are preparedness in disguise, embarking to obliterate the past, never to go home again. Battleships return for mental winter while rats leaving the ship are grateful for an opportunity to shine.

They amass a fortunate weapon, without the tourniquet of responsibility. Hegemony mixes with heresy to reveal a corpse of exquisite rationality. The many fragments of its garment's refractions dissolving in microbic mystery, before disappearing into structural hysteria, like a hamster weary of its wheel.

Hours reflect backwards in the hourglass of absence, as in a mirror's parallel recollection. If the minute recalls the messenger it doesn't tell. And if a crumb in time won't dissolve it's likely late for a previous engagement.

Photo finish the offspring before the enveloping tide. Forget the mission and forget the tide.

Exhale the finite glow of our forgotten planet. If only we had a parachute of elastic carbon to forestall its demise.

To be without a backdrop when there's no curtain, that's the imitation.

Too elusive to be apprehended by pursuing parables and forestalled by that very wicket that we tripped over to begin with. We are back at the start with only a cart and a wheel.

An inkling, a painted kaleidoscope background, identities changing with each generation. Quick, an upset! There is no costume to contain all the karma. Initiate a frozen setting. What are we waiting for? The masters are all asleep now.

AFTERWARD

Since the 1980s I've been keeping a journal of writing that I channel through a trance state. Only recently has the author revealed his name to me. *Telescope Highway* and my previous book, *Earth After Earth*, are collaborations with a group of entities, including one who calls himself Menippus. Through the years they have provided all the material; I've deciphered and reassembled it into a narrative thread. I was surprised to discover that there was an actual philosopher named Menippus born circa 300 BC. His writing has been completely lost — only the titles remain — including *Letters — artificially composed as if by the gods* and *Necromancy.*

Toni Simon is a multimedia artist and writer. Her
work encompasses the ways in which the future
might appear, the shape of things to come, accessed
through trance states. The process of channeled,
automatic writing led to Simon's illustrated book
and animated videos of experimental prose poetry
Earth After Earth, (Lunar Chandelier Press, 2012)
and to *Telescope Highway*. She lives in Brooklyn.